ĒRIKS EŠENVALDS

Choral Anthology 2

for mixed choir
(SATB)

in collaboration with

EIGENTUM DES VERLEGERS · ALLE RECHTE VORBEHALTEN
ALL RIGHTS RESERVED

PETERS EDITION LTD

A member of the EDITION PETERS GROUP
FRANKFURT/M. · LEIPZIG · LONDON · NEW YORK

This compilation © 2013 by Peters Edition Ltd, London

Peters Edition Ltd
2–6 Baches Street
London N1 6DN
www.editionpeters.com

CONTENTS

Amazing Grace. 5

Stars 15

Only in Sleep 20

In my Little Picture Frame. 28

Long Road. 37

Veltīts Rīgas Jauniešu korim Kamēr... / Dedicated to the Riga Youth Choir Kamēr...

AMAZING GRACE

John Newton
(1725-1807)

Traditional American tune
arranged by Ēriks Ešenvalds
(*1977)

© Copyright Musica Baltica, 2007

14 **poco allargando**

2004

Commissioned by the Salt Lake Vocal Artists / Salt Lake Choral Artists, Brady Allred, Conductor

STARS

Sara Teasdale · Ēriks Ešenvalds

✷ Choose resonant glasses and use as little water to tune them as possible - the less water, the more resonant the sound. There must be some water, however, as the glasses are played with wet fingertips. Every second singer plays a glass. The pitches of every glass-sound chord should be divided equally between the players. For bars 42-76 you may also add a few larger glass or Tibetan-type bowls with pitches D, E and A to add more lower sounds than the sounds produced by the glasses.

© Copyright *Musica Baltica* 2011

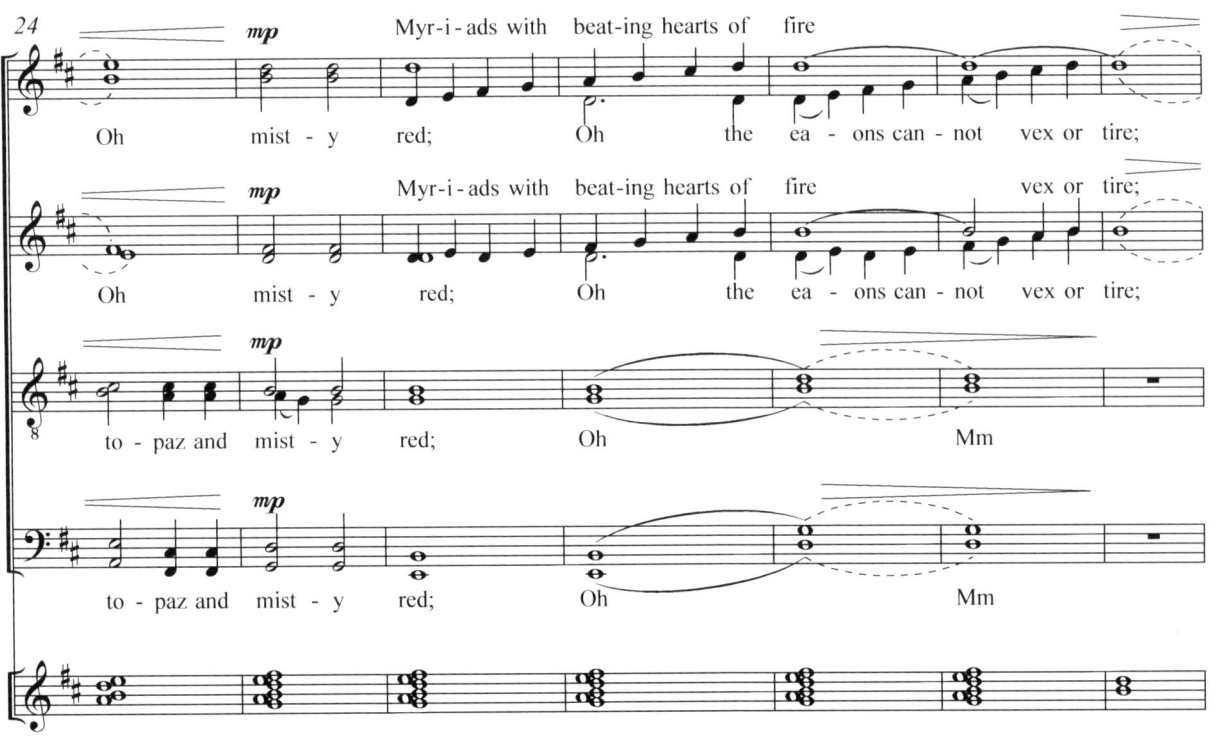

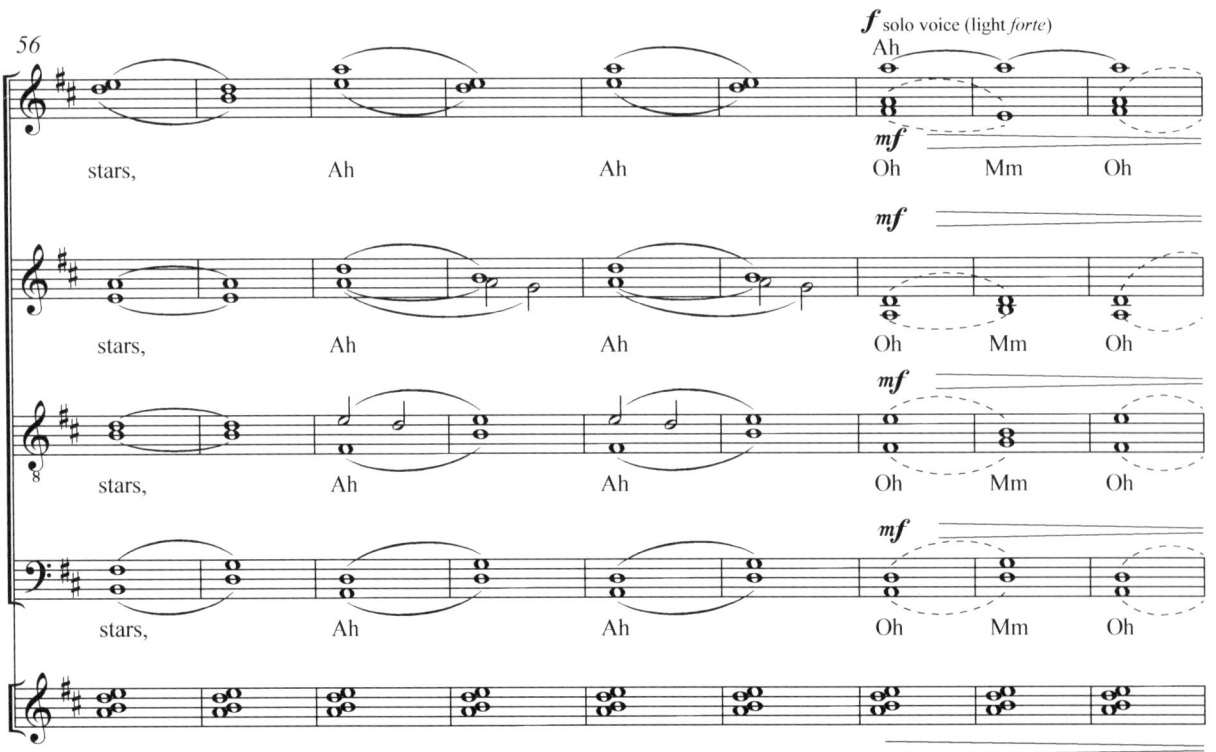

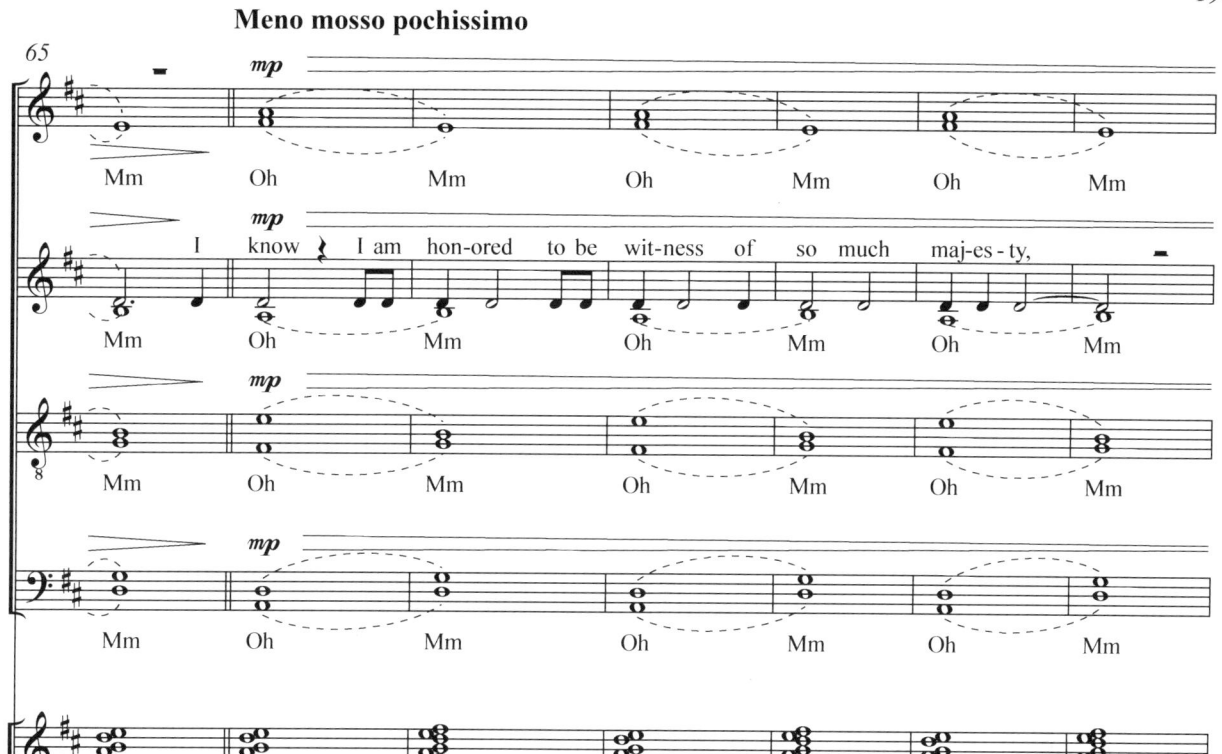
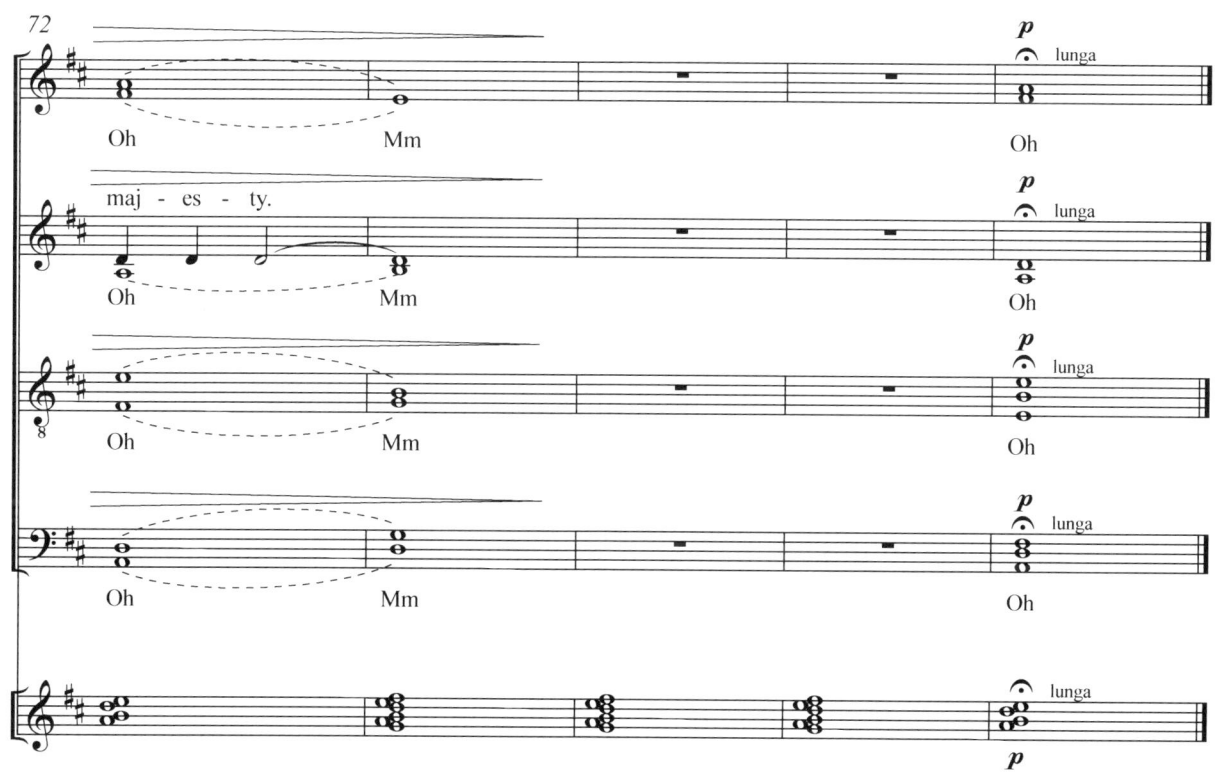

Commissioned by the University of Louisville Collegiate Chorale and Cardinal Singers. Conductor: Kent Hatteberg

ONLY IN SLEEP
TIKAI MIEGĀ

Sara Teasdale
(1884–1933)

Ēriks Ešenvalds
(*1977)

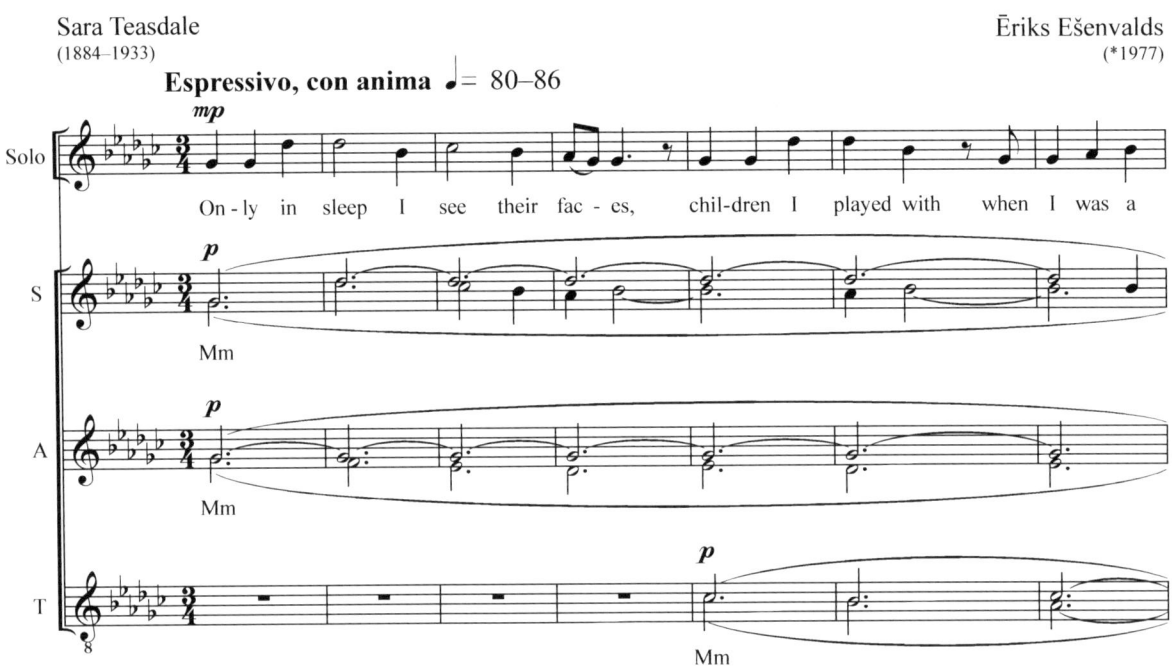

© Copyright Musica Baltica, 2012

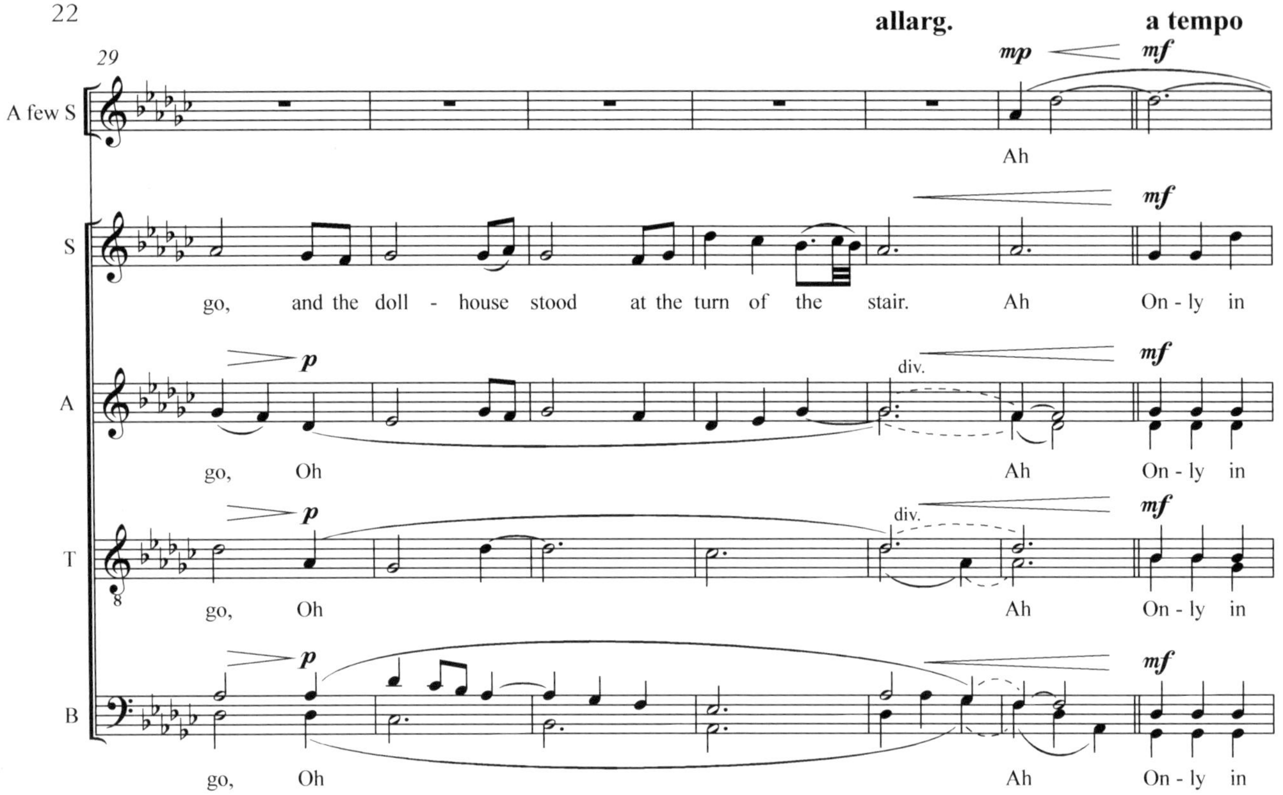
allarg.
a tempo
29
A few S
S
A
T
B
mp mf
p
div.
Ah
go, and the doll - house stood at the turn of the stair. Ah On - ly in
go, Oh Ah On - ly in
go, Oh Ah On - ly in
go, Oh Ah On - ly in

36
A few S
S
A
T
B
mf
unis.
div.
Ah
sleep I see their fac - es, chil-dren I played with when I was a child,
sleep I see their fac - es, chil-dren I played with when I was a child,
sleep I see their fac - es, chil-dren I played with when I was a child,
sleep I see their fac - es, chil-dren I played with when I was a child,

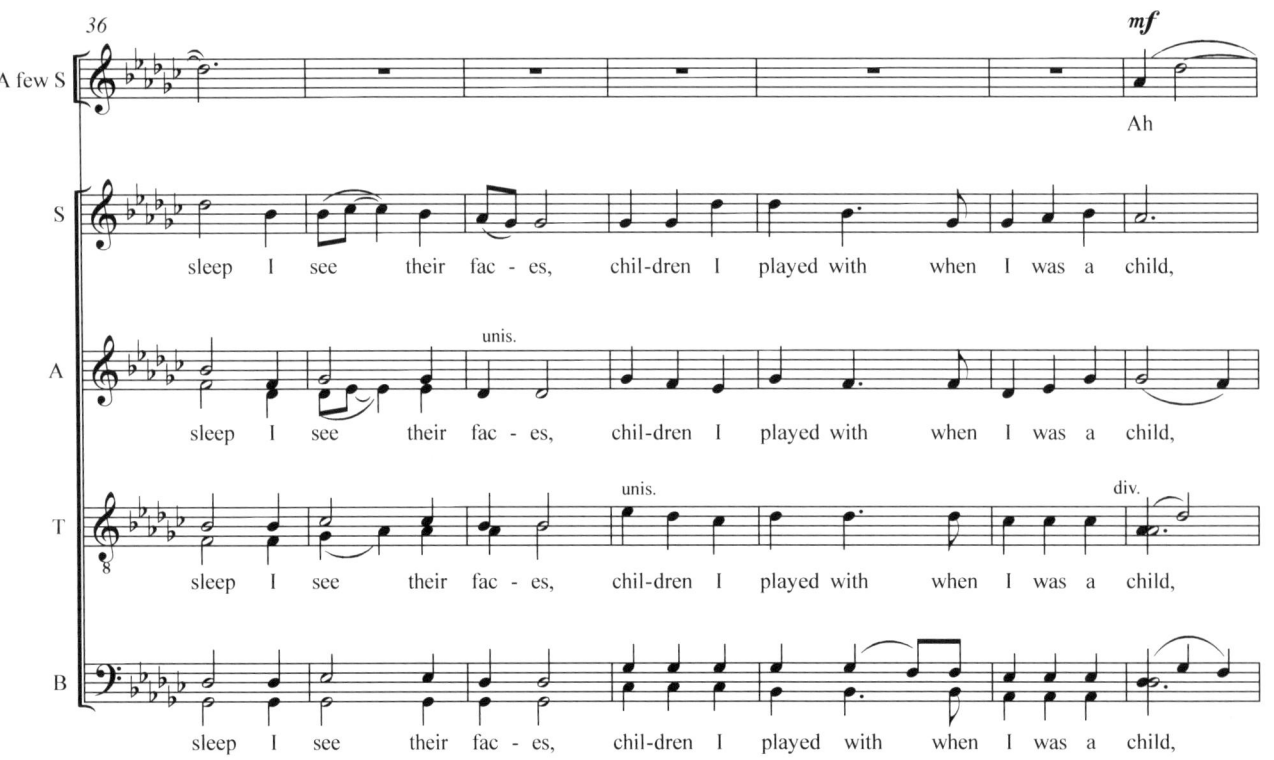

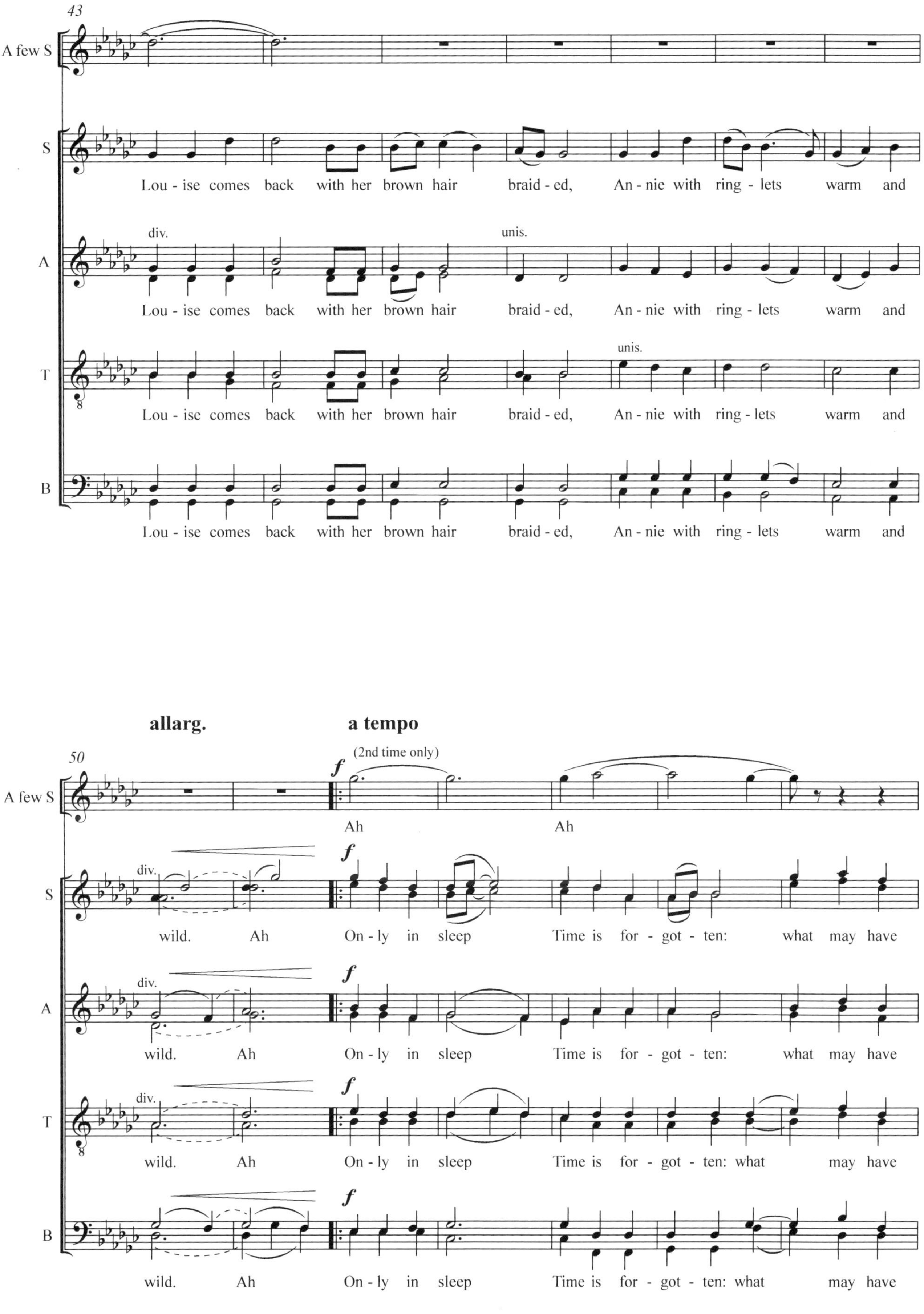
43
A few S
S
A
T
B
div.
unis.
unis.
Lou - ise comes back with her brown hair braid - ed, An - nie with ring - lets warm and
allarg.
a tempo
50
(2nd time only)
Ah
Ah
wild. Ah
On - ly in sleep Time is for - got - ten: what may have
On - ly in sleep Time is for - got - ten: what may have
wild. Ah
div.
f

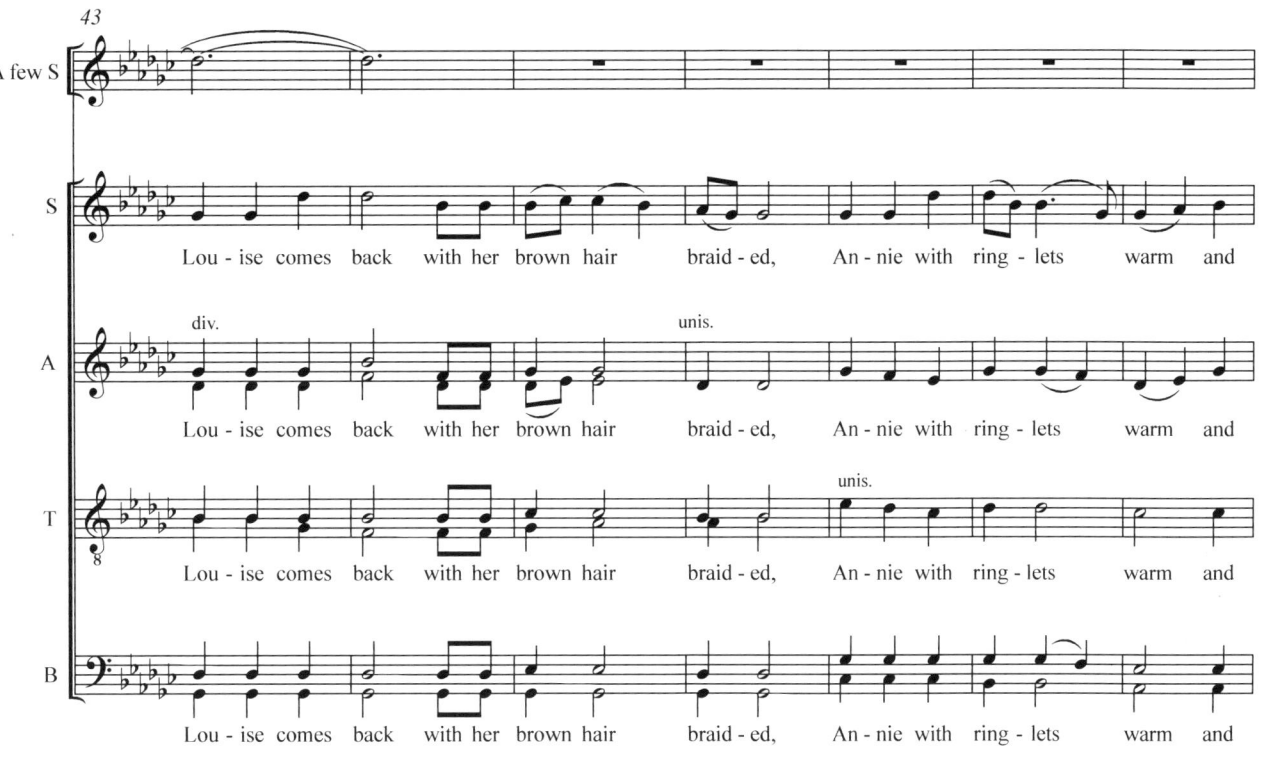

57
A few S
S
A
T
B
(1st and 2nd time)
mf
unis.
Ah
come to them, who can know? Yet we played last night as long a -

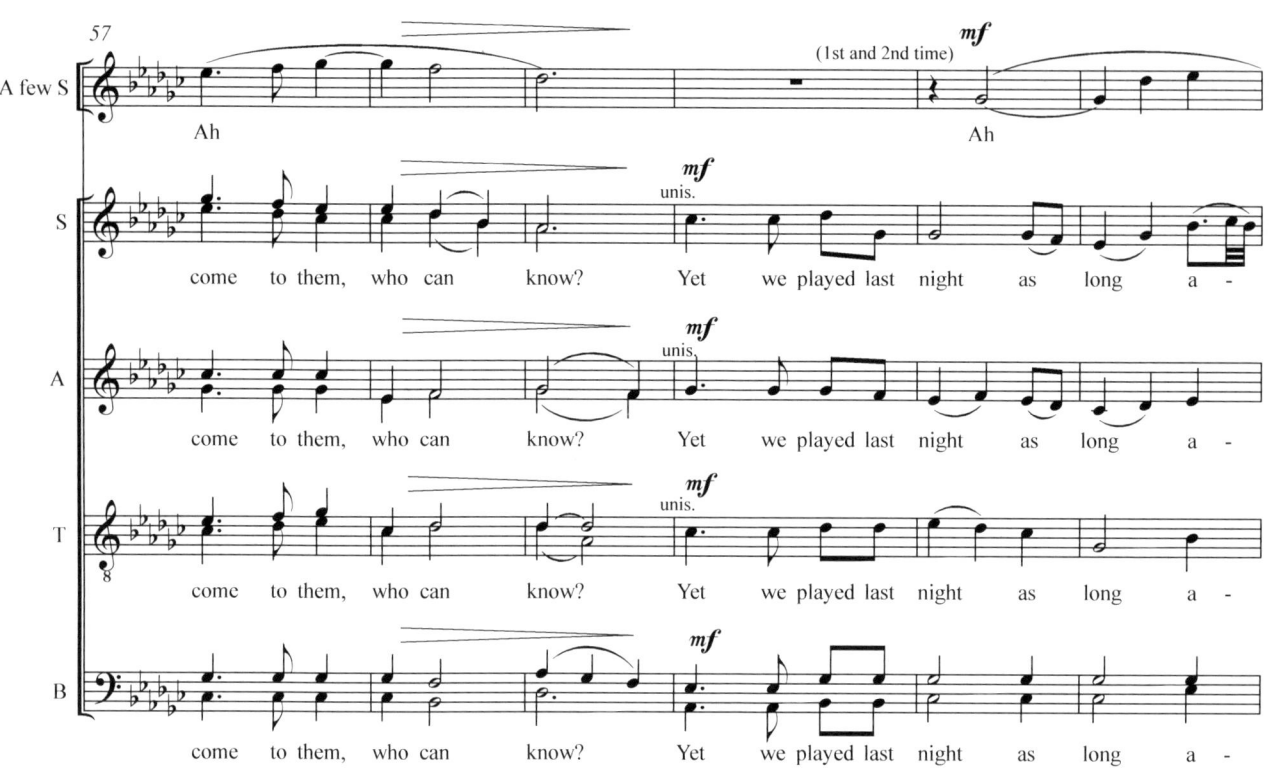

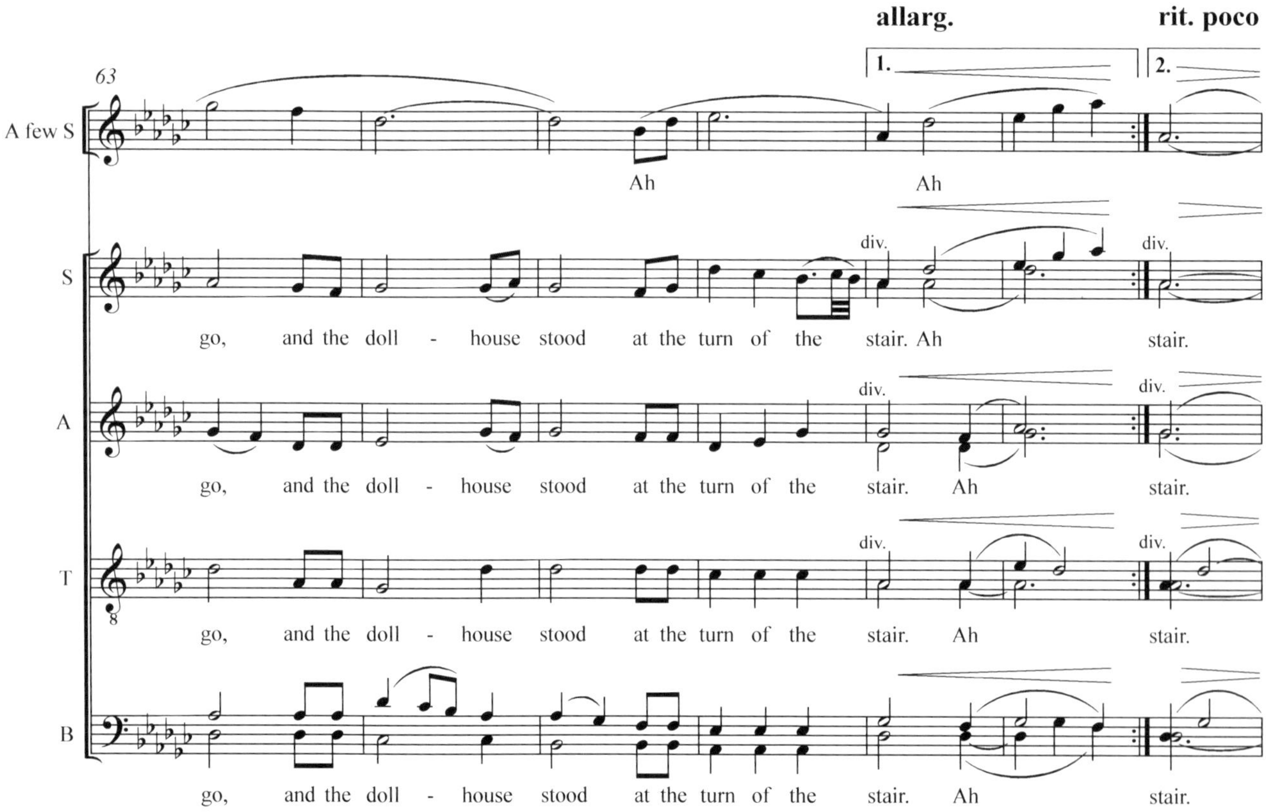
allarg.
rit. poco
63
1.
2.
div.
Ah
go, and the doll - house stood at the turn of the stair. Ah
stair.

70
a tempo
mp
Solo
The years had not sharp-ened their smooth round fac - es, I met their eyes and
A few S
S
p
Mm
A
p
Mm
T
p
ppp p
Mm
Mm
B
p
ppp
Mm
77
Solo
found them mild. Do they, too, dream of me, I won - der, and for them
S
mp
Mm
Ah
A
mp
Mm
Ah
T
mp
Mm
Ah
B
mp
Mm
Ah

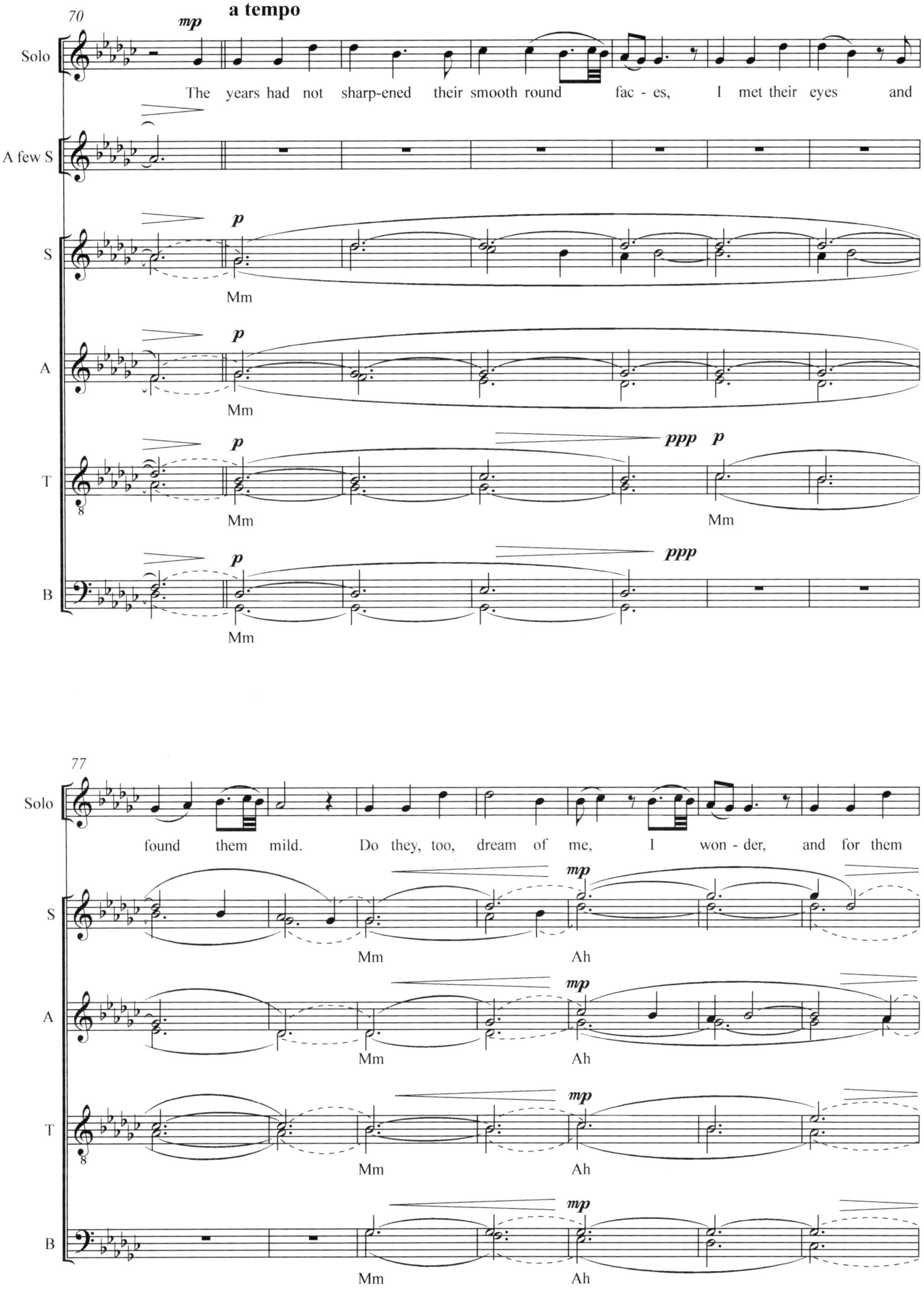

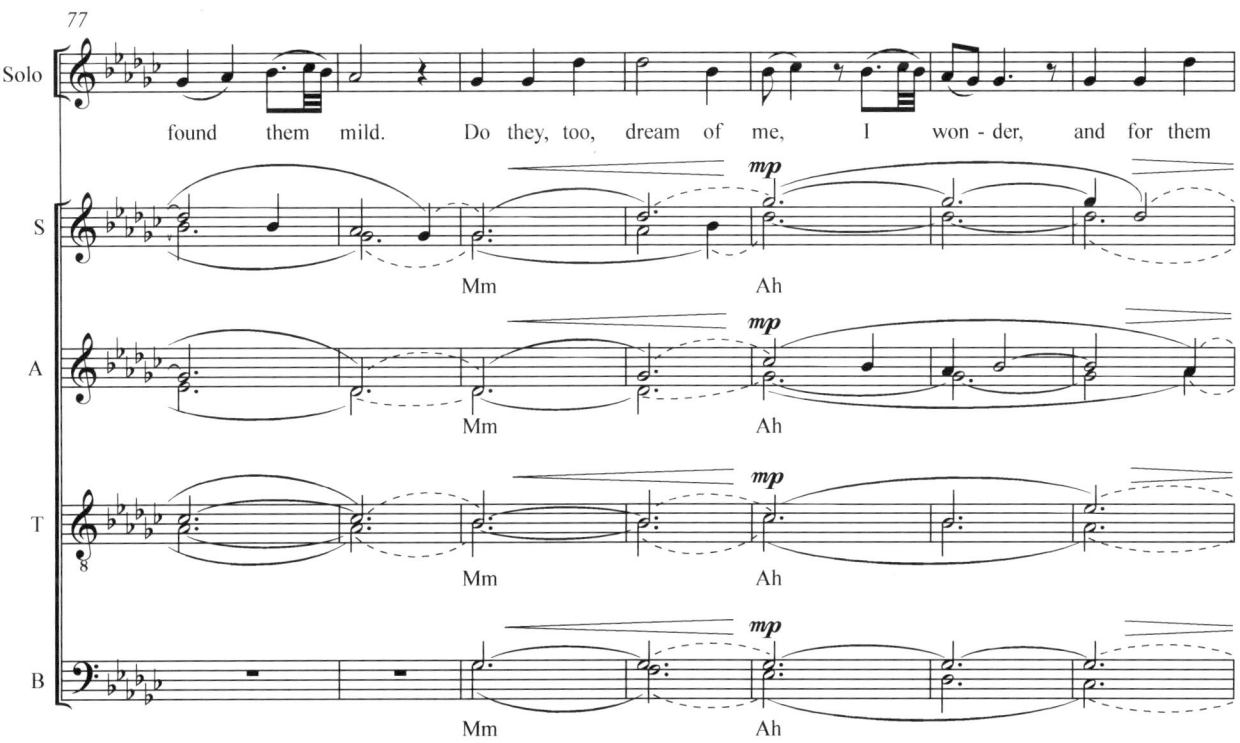

IN MY LITTLE PICTURE FRAME

Lyrics by Imants Ziedonis
(*1933)
English transl. by Ieva Lešinska-Geiber
and Elaine Singley Lloyd

Music by Renārs Kaupers
(*1974)
Arranged by Ēriks Ešenvalds
(*1977)

Con amore ♩= 108–112
pp

S I: baM — baM baM baM pa ra baM — baM baM baM baM
S II: ba da baM — ba da baM ba da ba daM — ba da baM ba da ba daM
S III: ba da baM ba d ba daM ba da baM ba da baM ba da baM
A I: ba daM ba daM ba daM ba daM ba daM baM baM baM — baM baM
A II: baM baM — baM — baM baM ba daM ba daM ba da ba da ba daM

T:
In my lit - tle
It's a qui - et

© Copyright Musica Baltica 2011

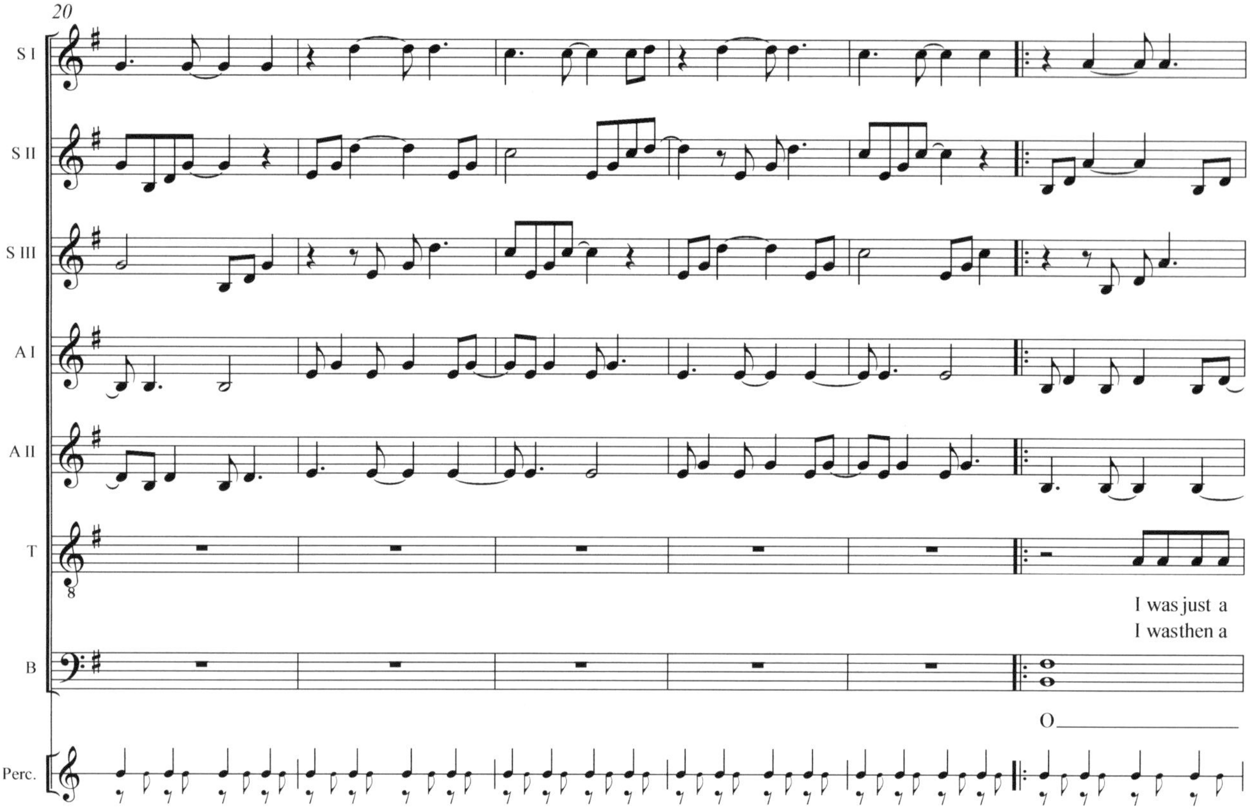
20
S I
S II
S III
A I
A II
T
I was just a
I wasthen a
B
O
Perc.

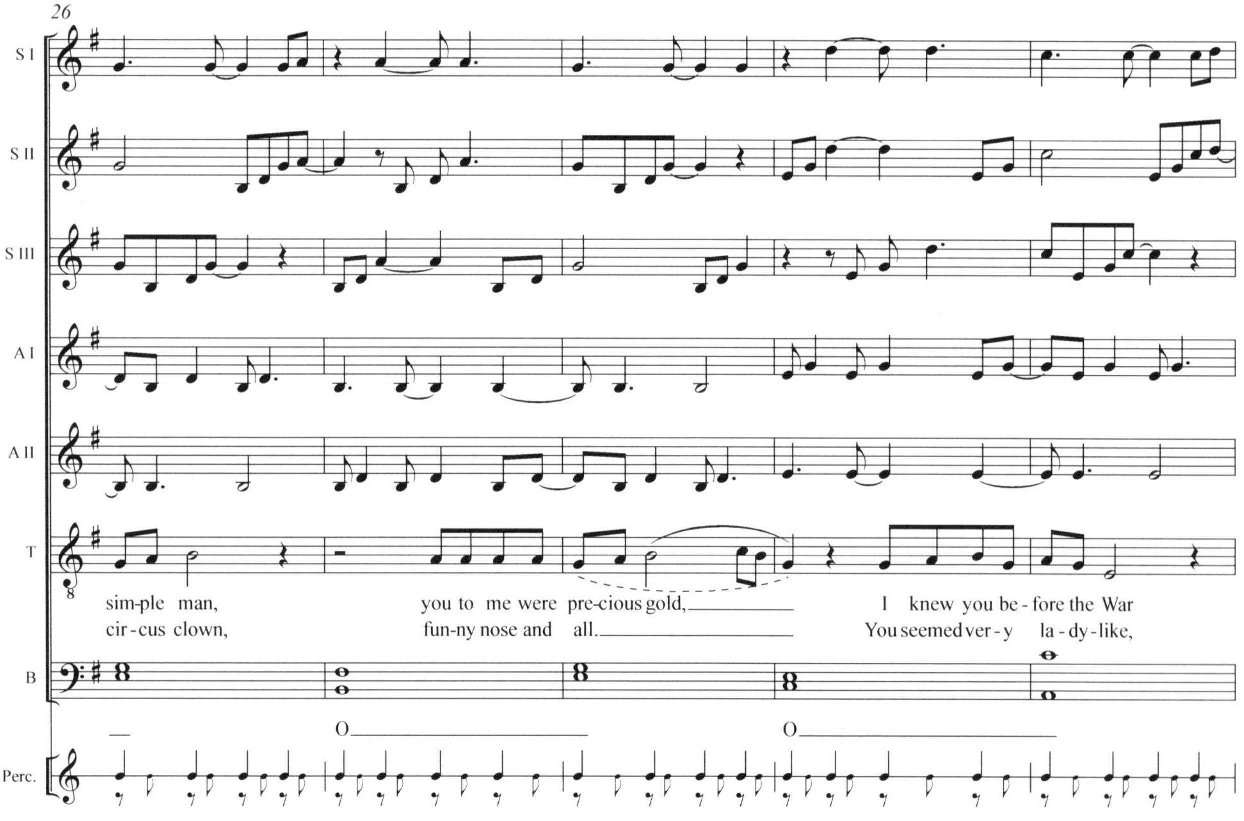
26
S I
S II
S III
A I
A II
T
sim-ple man, you to me were pre-cious gold, I knew you be-fore the War
cir-cus clown, fun-ny nose and all. You seemed ver-y la-dy-like,
B
O O
Perc.

Long Road is the English version of my recent choral composition *Tāls ceļš* (text by Latvian poet Paulīne Bārda), and it is dedicated to Stephen Layton and *Polyphony* who first performed it on April 8th, 2010 in Trinity College Chapel Cambridge.

LONG ROAD

Paulīne Bārda
(1890-1983)
English transl. by Elaine Singley Lloyd

Ēriks Ešenvalds
(*1977)

© Copyright MUSICA BALTICA 2010

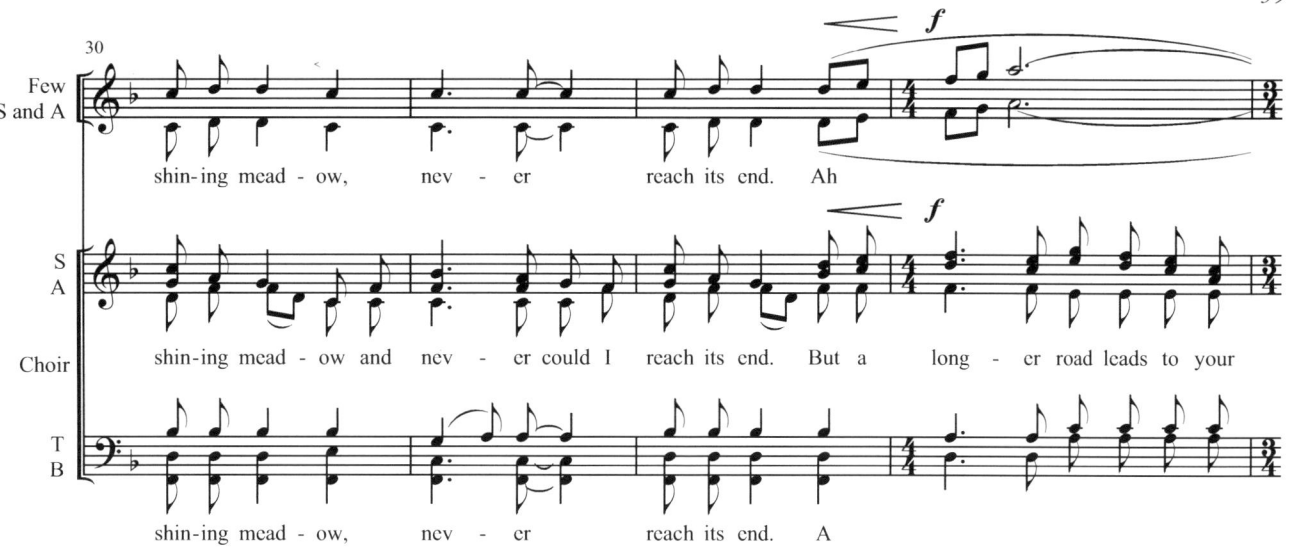
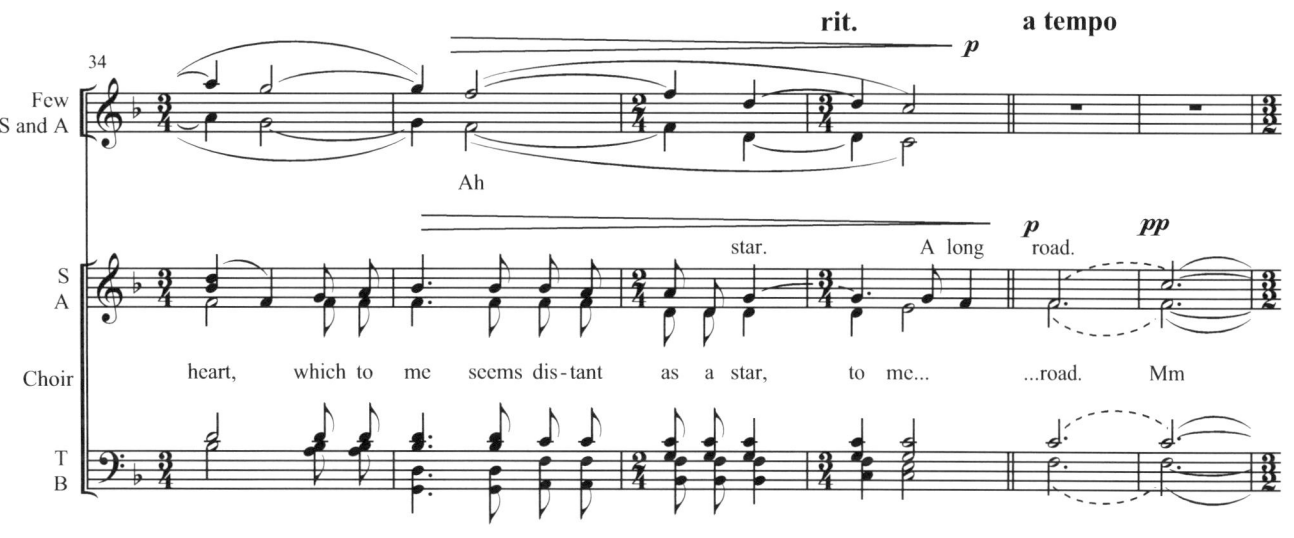
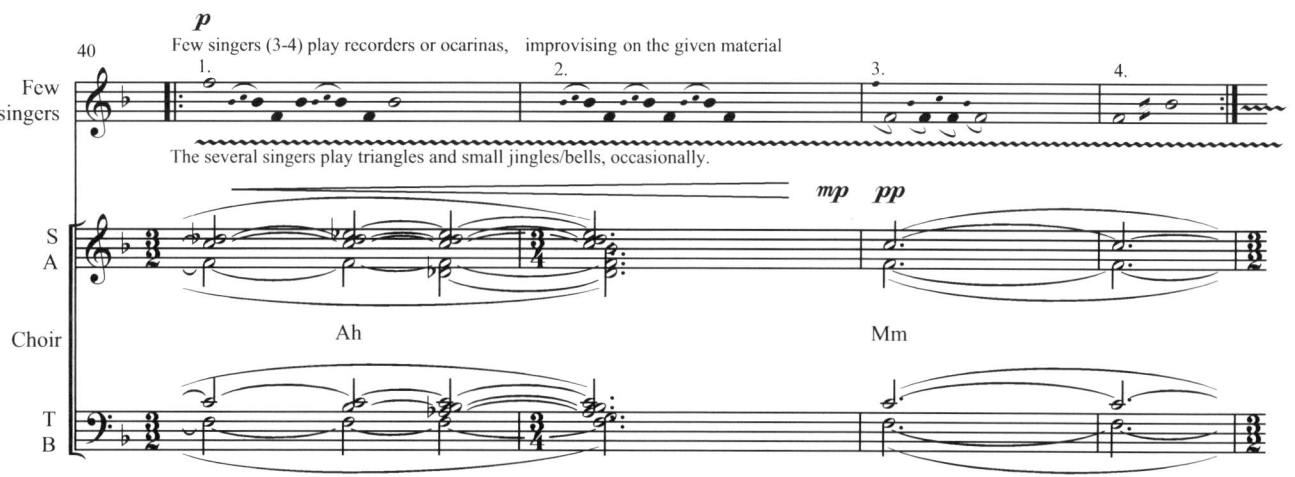

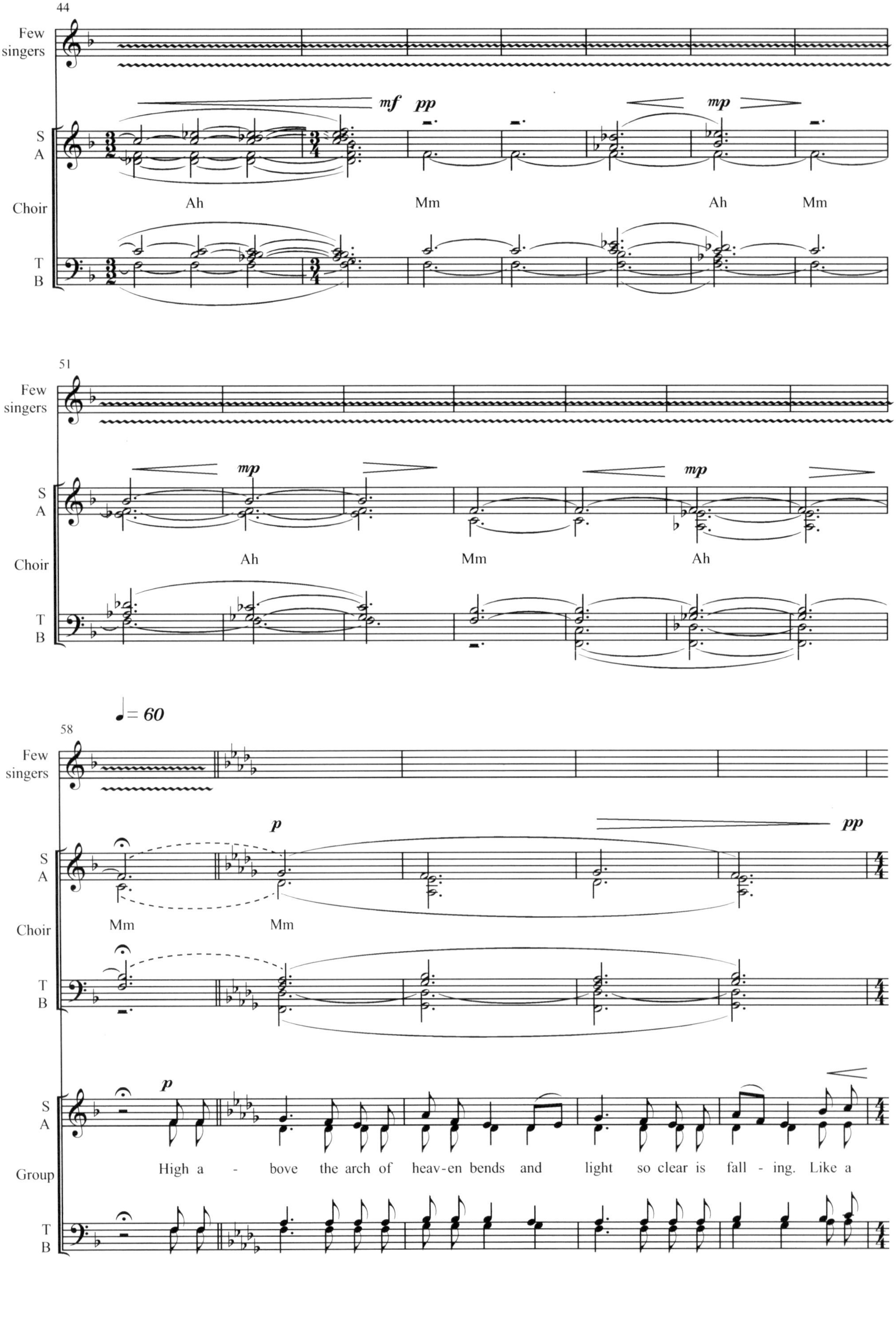

44
Few singers
S A
Choir
T B
mf pp mp
Ah
Mm
Ah
Mm
51
mp
Ah
Mm
Ah
♩= 60
58
p
pp
Mm
Mm
Group
High a - bove the arch of heav-en bends and light so clear is fall - ing. Like a